To

From

Date

COVENANT KEEPER, NOT A COVENANT BREAKER

Enjoying Daily Manifestation Of God's Promises

THE CORNERSTONE PUBLISHING

Yemi Oyinkansola

Covenant Keeper, Not a Covenant Breaker

Enjoying daily manifestation of God's Promises

Copyright © 2018 by **Yemi Oyinkansola**

Paperback ISBN: 978-1-952098-06-2

Printed in the United States of America. All rights reserved solely by the publisher. This book or parts thereof may not be reproduced in any form, stored in a retrieval system, or transmitted in any form by any means - electronic, mechanical, photocopy. Unless otherwise noted, Bible quotations are taken from the Holy Bible, King James Version. Copyright 1982 by Thomas Nelson, Inc., publishers. Used by permission.

Published by:
Cornerstone Publishing
A Division of Cornerstone Creativity Group LLC
Info@thecornerstonepublishers.com
www.thecornerstonepublishers.com
516.547.4999

Author's Contact

For speaking engagement or to order books by Pastor Yemi Oyinkansola:

Info@yemioyinkansola.com
www.yemioyinkansola.com
+1 510.258.4583

DEDICATION

Specially dedicated to:

- My Lord and Savior, Jesus Christ, the Covenant Giver and Covenant Keeper.
- All Covenant believers and unbelievers that will read this book and believe in the Covenant-Keeping God.
- All my mentors and protégées in the Faith
- All members of Jesus House, Antioch, California.
- All my family members and friends in the faith.

ACKNOWLEDGMENTS

I thank God Almighty for giving me the title and the inspiration for this book. I specially thank and appreciate my beautiful wife, Comfort, and my lovely children, Melody and Toluwani, for their love, care and support always. Daddy really loves you guys.

I appreciate my staff at Jesus House, Antioch - Pastor Kay, Sister Justina Udoh Okon and Brother Jason Pfeiffer - for always making new things happen.

I appreciate all my ministers, workers and members at JHA in California for believing in the Covenant Keeping God and for believing in the call of God over my life. You all are the best. I'm so proud of you guys.

Thank you Pastor Gbenga Showunmi from Cornerstone Creativity Group. Your input into this work is huge.

Yemi Oyinkansola
September, 2018

CONTENTS

Dedication..5
Acknowledgments..7
Introduction...11
1. God is Not a Man..13
2. Covenant: What is it?..27
3. God, The Covenant Maker..................................37
4. God, The Covenant Keeper.................................53
5. Keeping Your Side of the Bargain.......................67
6. Timing is Key..77
7. Covenant Promises for Every Situation...............89
About Yemi Oyinkansola...97

INTRODUCTION

Shortly before his ascension to heaven, Jesus asked a poignant question that must have had little meaning to those who initially heard it but which has now proved to be full of insight and power, just like all of His other sayings. That question is, *"When the Son of man comes, will he really find faith on the earth?" (Luke 18:8)*.

As we consider the attitude of many believers today to the word of God and the promises they once held so dear, the truth of this inquiry becomes more evident. We are living in particularly challenging times - not just because of the numerous darts of difficulties that we have to contend with but because of the barrage of pressure to compromise our faith and resort to shortcuts and quick fixes to overcome these challenges. And it is no surprise that nearly on daily basis, we get reports of children of God abandoning the faith in their desperation to cope with the demands of daily life.

Even among those who haven't abandoned the faith yet, many are just barely hanging on in helpless resignation.

They're not totally out but they are not fully in either. Generally, there's a high level of despair and anxiety, with many doubting the wisdom of trusting in the same God who has proved to be a sure anchor and succor for many generations of believers.

The main question is, what has changed over the years? Is it God who has changed? Or, may we ask, like Jeremiah, *"Is there no more balm in Gilead?" (Jeremiah 8:22)*. Of course, it is not God who has changed; it is His children, who, like Peter, are increasingly turning their gaze from the Lord and His words, and paying more attention to the lies of Satan and the illusions of the world.

God has not changed and will never change. His purpose, love, care, concern and faithfulness towards His children remain the same yesterday, today and forever. Those who have chosen to fix their eyes and faith on Him, regardless of circumstances, negative reports or even the discouraging attitudes of other believers, have continued to testify of His unfailing commitment to His promises, as well as His unlimited power to deliver in all situations.

As you read this book, this is the same request the Lord making of you: *"Look to Me, and be saved…For I am God, and there is no other" (Isaiah 45:22).*

CHAPTER 1

GOD IS NOT A MAN

On February 28, 2018, the Nigerian Guardian newspaper captioned its editorial with the screaming headline: Promise Makers, Promise Breakers. It then went on to detail how the country's political leaders, just like their predecessors, had broken many of the promises made to the populace during the electioneering campaigns.

As I began to write this book, I recalled this editorial and decided to scour the Internet for what newspapers in other countries were saying about their leaders and I wasn't surprised that the lamentations of broken promises and failed expectations were a global malady. Yet, the deeper truth is that unfaithfulness to promises and covenants is not just the hallmark of politicians; it is an intrinsic nature of the fallen man, the manifestation of which has reached alarming proportions in our world in recent times.

Look around you and you will find glaring proofs that covenant-keeping seems to have been deleted from the human vocabulary and moral code. People break covenants at will without caring for the consequences. Marriage vows and covenants are broken in a matter of days. There are even websites dedicated to promoting and glorifying adultery, with millions of members from all over the world. Family and friendship covenants are also being broken without any remorse. Same goes for business agreements, contracts and conditions which are being daily violated, without any sense of shame from the perpetrators.

NO EXCEPTIONS

If you are appalled by the state of things as described above, then wait for this. Nowadays, it has become so shameful that even among supposed believers and covenant children of God, there is no difference in attitude towards covenants and agreements. In fact, it is even worse, in some instances, to have a deal or transact a business with so-called people of God. Agreements, contracts and regulations are broken at will even in the church of God. From the pulpit to the pew, there is general disregard for God's covenant.

As if to confirm this fact, some years back, George Gallup (founder of the Gallup poll) conducted a survey on ethical behavior in workplaces around America, and the findings were disturbing. According to him, "We find there is very little difference in ethical behavior between churchgoers and those who are not active religiously. The levels of lying, cheating, and stealing are remarkably similar in both groups."

Thus, having been used to the sight, sound and stench of unfaithfulness all around for so long, it has become so easy for many of us to fall into the trap of having the same idea of God – that it is possible for God, just like men, to either forget His covenants or renege on performing them altogether. This is the root of the anxiety and perplexity that manifest in the lives of many believers and the church as a whole today, leading many to sometimes cut corners and seeking shortcut solutions which they end up regretting.

A TIMELY REMINDER

It is for this reason that, in looking at the subject of God as the Covenant Keeper, we must begin by reminding ourselves that there is absolutely no basis of comparison between the Almighty God and mortal men. God is not man. God is everything that man is not. This would seem obvious already, but it is not enough for us to see this difference as we would think of two different personalities. No, this is a difference between a creature and the Creator, between mortality and immortality, between limitation and infiniteness, between impotence and omnipotence. When we have this understanding deeply engraved on our minds, it will revolutionize our perception of God and our attitudes towards the covenants He makes with us.

Therefore, we must be fully persuaded that regardless

of what we might have been used to with our fellow men, including fellow Christians, our relationship with God is on another level entirely. And it is on this basis that we must approach Him and view everything He says to us. I will shortly be pointing out specific instances of this infinite incomparability between man and God, to show you why we must learn to do away with any suggestion of unfaithfulness when it comes to God.

EXTRAORDINARY ENCOUNTER

By the way, in case you have not noticed, the heading of this chapter is directly taken from a verse of the Scripture. The entire verse says,

> *"God is not a man, that He should lie, Nor a son of man, that He should repent. Has He said, and will He not do? Or has He spoken, and will He not make it good?"* (Numbers 23:19).

This is one of the most reassuring Scripture verses and one which every believer ought to commit to memory. However, I need to let you know the background to the verse, not just because it is interesting, instructive and inspiring but also because it is very much illustrative of the message that the Holy Spirit wants to inscribe in your mind through this book.

Here is the summary. Hundreds of years after God had made a covenant with Abraham and promised him that His descendants would be exceedingly blessed and would inherit the land of Canaan, it was time for the fulfillment. The Israelites had just been wondrously liberated from the captivity of the Egyptians, after over 400 years of enslavement – which God had also previously told Abraham – and were on their way to possessing the covenanted land. Just then, Balak, the king of Moab, one of the lands the Israelites were to pass through, became alarmed, after hearing all that God had done for and through His people. So, he hired Balaam, a renowned diviner, who was known to have special powers to pronounce curses, to help him curse the Israelites.

Well, Balaam tried and failed because there was something much stronger than any curse in place – the covenant of blessing. Again and again, the two men tried, changing from location to location, building altar to altar; yet nothing could displace the covenant of blessing upon the Israelites. In fact, rather than succeeding in pronouncing a curse on them, Balaam found himself affirming and amplifying the blessing of God upon them, with powerful prophetic utterances, which confounded Balak himself. It was in the process of making the utterances that he uttered the verse we are considering, the message of which is not only for Balak but for Balaam himself and, most importantly, for us today.

Before we consider this message, it might interest you more to know that the Israelites were totally unaware of all that was going on between Balak and Balaam. In other words, while they were going about their daily routines, there were forces working behind the scenes to frustrate God's purpose for their lives. Yet, the conspiracy of the enemy could not prevail because of the potency of the covenant. Essentially, even when they were not in the know, God was keeping to His side of the bargain.

I will be talking more about God keeping to His side of the bargain in a later chapter. But for now, we must consider the message that God intended for us in the verse. This event reveals the following salient truths about the nature of God that should guide our attitude towards His covenants and promises.

1. GOD DOES NOT CHANGE

This is one truth that Balak and Balaam probably did not know. And this is what many of us professing believers seem not know either, which is why we worry and fret about life's battles and challenges, when our minds should be at rest. As I mentioned already, the event in this verse took place several hundreds of years after the initial covenant had been made with Abraham. Yet, God remained committed to His promise. Balaam, being experienced in the craft of divination, probably knew about the special place that the Israelites occupied in God's program, a reason he didn't want to go with Balak in the first place (Numbers 22:7-18). However, being a man, he soon gave in to pressure out of greed for filthy lucre.

Indeed, men change over time. Time does things to men, not only physically but mentally and behaviorally. And this, of course, affects their attitude to their vows and pledges. Sometimes when I see a couple going through a divorce and especially a bitter one, the first thing that occurs to me is, wasn't there a time when these people promised to love and care for each other forever? Wasn't there a time when they seemed never to be able to get enough of each other? What happened between then and now? Change – occasioned by time and circumstances.

Cheeringly, our God is not this way. God is not a man that He should change. He says in Malachi 3:6,

> *"For I am the Lord, I do not change; Therefore, you are not consumed, O sons of Jacob."*

This is one assurance that should give us comfort in all circumstances. The Ancient of Days is the same yesterday, today and forever. Unlike man, He is not affected by time, age, mood or circumstances. This is why He is described as "The Rock" in Deuteronomy 32:4. A rock remains unmoved, even as the ocean all around it fluctuates according to the dictates of the wind. As A.W. Pink puts it, "Because God has no beginning and no ending, He can know no change". His promises to you are ever binding.

It does not matter how many times men have failed and disappointed you; it does not matter how many times men have broken your heart; God's love for you is everlasting. He says to you to comfort and assure you:

> *"I have loved you with an everlasting love; Therefore, with lovingkindness I have drawn you. Again I will build you, and you shall be rebuilt…" (Jeremiah 31:3-4).*

You will find a handy instance of God's immutability in His care for His children in the same encounter between Balak and Balaam. I mentioned earlier that Israel was not aware of the devilish scheming between these two men, yet God's protection over His people remained unshakeable. What this means is that God's care for you is not dependent on how much you're able to fret yourself or how much fire you have in your spirit. Sometimes you are able to pray for an hour and sometimes it could just be a minute, yet the mercies of God upon your life are new every morning. It is for this reason that Matthew Henry, in his commentary on the verse, says, "Men change their minds, and break their words; but God never changes his mind, and therefore never recalls his promise."

2. GOD DOES NOT LIE

Yes, men do lie - whether it is with the intention of outright deception or simply to save face. It is a major part of the nature of Satan that the fallen man inherited. Satan is the father of lies and the unregenerate man is under the dominion of Satan. This is why Jesus said to the religious people of His day:

> "You are of your father the devil, and the desires of your father you want to do. He was a murderer from the beginning, and does not stand in the truth, because there is no truth in him. When he speaks a lie, he speaks from his own resources, for he is a liar and the father of it" (John 8:44).

It is thus natural for man, having been used to lies and

deceit, either from personal failings or from the actions of others, to see lying as a normal practice, even if it's occasional. But God is not a man. He means everything He says and says only what He means. He has no nature of the devil in Him, nor is He subject to his temptations - and so it is impossible for Him to tell a lie. 1 John 1:5 says, "This is the message which we have heard from Him and declare to you, that God is light and in Him is no darkness at all."

Hebrews 6:18-19 is even more direct:

> *"That by two immutable things, in which it is impossible for God to lie, we might have strong consolation, who have fled for refuge to lay hold of the hope set before us. This hope we have as an anchor of the soul, both sure and steadfast, and which enters the Presence behind the veil..."*

This is a solid anchor for every believer. We serve a God whose every utterance and every assurance can be relied upon in every situation of life. This confidence is powerful enough to nullify everything that contradicts God's declarations and promises for your life. Believers down the ages who have understood the efficacy of this sure anchor have obtained unprecedented victories, wrought extraordinary wonders, overturned Satanic conspiracies, and countered negative verdicts and diagnoses. Indeed, some have gone as far as altering the course of nature – just because they believed that

> *"let God be true but every man (and circumstance) a liar" (Romans 3:4).*

What do you think made Joshua to be able to boldly

declare that the sun and moon should stand still, till the people of God had overcome all their adversaries (Joshua 10)? What do you think made Elijah to be able to confidently declare to Ahab, the wicked king, that there would be no rain in Israel for three-and-a-half years, except according to his word (1 Kings 17:1)? It's simply because God had given them the word and they believed that the words of the God who can NEVER lie supersedes every other word or event.

3. GOD DOES NOT FORGET

Since, unlike man, God is neither rash in making promises nor does He make promises under compulsion, He does not forget them. It does not matter how long His words take to come to fulfillment, it's never a sign of forgetfulness. Man may forget their words and vows, perhaps because of the hustle-bustle and cares of life, but God never does. Every one of His children matters to Him and He takes their affairs very seriously.

Yet, being humans who are used to forgetting our promises or who have had people forgetting their promises to us, we sometimes tend to think that delay in the fulfillment of God's promises or will for our lives means that He has forgotten us. The Israelites once made this error too. Isaiah 59:14 records:

> "Zion said, The Lord has forsaken me, and my Lord has forgotten me."

But God's answer to them and to us today is: "Can a woman forget her nursing child, and not have compassion on the son of her womb? Surely they may forget, yet I will not forget you. See, I have inscribed you on the palms of My hands; Your walls are continually before Me."

What a marvelous and compassionate Father we have! Be sure of it – He has not and can NEVER forget you or any of His words to you. Heaven and earth may pass away, but not the least of what God has declared for your life will go without fulfillment. To show you how serious He is about what affects you, He says He has carved (note, not written, but CARVED) your name on the palms of His hands and everything about your life is ever before Him. How then can you think you could be forgotten for even a second!

4. GOD IS NOT LIMITED IN ABILITY

Men sometimes make promises that they find difficult to fulfill because ability fails them. There are even times when the promise-maker starts on a good note but soon begins to renege and indeed begins to regret making the promise in the first place. It may be because the need has grown bigger than imagined or that the means of meeting it has diminished. Praise be to our God that He is not like that. There is no need that He cannot meet. Nothing can go beyond the scope of His ability or the reach of His authority. There is nothing He says that He cannot accomplish. He has the power to say and to do – which no human being can guarantee.

In fact, being the Almighty, the moment God utters a

word concerning your life, He doesn't have to begin to struggle or strain Himself to bring it to pass; instead, the forces of accomplishment are instantly set in motion by the word. As it was in the time of the creation, everything – people, situations, circumstances – begin to respond and gravitate in the direction of what has been declared. This is why God says in Isaiah 55:10-11,

> *"For as the rain comes down, and the snow from heaven, and do not return there, but water the earth, and make it bring forth and bud, that it may give seed to the sower and bread to the eater, so shall My word be that goes forth from My mouth; it shall not return to Me void, but it shall accomplish what I please, and it shall prosper in the thing for which I sent it."*

With God, there is no impossibility. There are no hopeless cases. He is the maker and sovereign ruler of the universe and so nothing gets outside of His control. No wonder that Prophet Jeremiah, having experienced God in this manner, confidently declared:

> *"Ah, Lord God! Behold, You have made the heavens and the earth by Your great power and outstretched arm. There is nothing too hard for You" (Jeremiah 32:17).*

So, cheer up, believer. God is not a man. Whatever He says, He can do and He will do. Let this assure you, despite the twists and turns of life. God's power, which is at work in your life and destiny, remains unchanging and unchallengeable!

5. GOD IS NOT SUBJECT TO THE LIMITATIONS OF MORTALITY

To be fair to mankind, there are times when an individual makes a promise and sincerely wishes to fulfill it. However, the limitations of mortality incapacitate him and turn the same person who has promised to be a giver of help to be a desperate seeker of help himself. What this means is than men, being mortal, are prone to many circumstances that are beyond their control. They may have good intentions, but the vicissitudes of life and unforeseen circumstances soon overturn their plans. I know of a father who promised his son to be there for him throughout his academic pursuits. However, by the time the son was ready to soar academically, the father had become too ill to even recognize him!

But then again, GOD IS NOT A MAN – which means that He is not subject to the travails and troubles that often render men helpless and compel them to go back on their promises. I love the way that C.D. Cole explains this distinctive attribute of God. He says: "He is never at the end of Himself. His resources are never diminished. He never faces an emergency. He knows nothing of crises. He never resorts to any new deal, for His plans and purposes are all eternal. Wisdom designed all His plans, and His power executes them, therefore "Known unto God are all his works from the beginning of the world" (Acts 15:18). There never was a time when God wondered what He would or could do. He has no experiment station where He learns what is best, for He naturally knows what is best. In all these points, man is in striking contrast to God. We are straitened in ourselves, often at our wit's end and helpless. We are limited in power and wisdom. We are limited in time, but God is the King of Eternity."

As I wrap up this chapter, I am inspired to return to the passage from which its heading was taken and reel out the promises there because they are meant for every child of God as they were meant for the Israelites. And it doesn't matter what your situation is currently; it doesn't matter what report you have heard or the number of people against you. Here is God's assurance for you and I want you to declare every part of it for yourself (input your name where necessary):

> *"God is not a man, that He should lie, nor a son of man, that He should repent. Has He said, and will He not do? Or has He spoken, and will He not make it good? ..."He has not observed iniquity in Jacob, Nor has He seen wickedness in Israel. The Lord his God is with him, And the shout of a King is among them. God brings them out of Egypt; He has strength like a wild ox. "For there is no sorcery against Jacob, Nor any divination against Israel. It now must be said of Jacob And of Israel, 'Oh, what God has done!'" (Numbers 23:19-23).*

CHAPTER 2

COVENANT: WHAT IS IT?

Now that we have established the nature of the One making covenants with us, we need to understand the nature of a covenant itself. To many people, the word "covenant", is one that evokes feelings of dread. This is because, contrary to God's original purpose, Satan and his agents have often used covenants as a means of enslavement and destruction. However, as we shall soon see, covenants should actually arouse feelings of gratitude, hope, comfort and strength in us.

Covenants are essential components of our lives because human life fundamentally revolves around relationships. Fostering, strengthening, sustaining and benefitting from these relationships often invariably require some form of agreement, written or unwritten. As the Scripture asks,

> *"Can two walk together, unless they are agreed?" (Amos 3:3).*

At the basic level then, you can think of a covenant as a bond between two or more parties who are bound together in a contractual agreement or relationship. Such agreement defines their essential obligations and commitments to each other. It can be an agreement between a husband and wife, a friendship pact between two people, an alliance between two nations, or an agreement between God and humans. John Owen describes it as "an absolute agreement between distinct persons, about the order and dispensing of things in their power, unto their mutual concern and advantage." A.W Pink calls it "the entering into of a mutual agreement, a benefit being assured on the fulfilment of certain conditions."

Thus, a covenant presupposes two or more parties who come together to make a contract, agreeing on promises, stipulations, privileges, and responsibilities.

Covenants can be categorized into three major groups – human, satanic and divine. By human covenants, I mean covenants entered into by two or more human parties. By satanic covenants, I mean covenants between a human party and a satanic one, especially the demonic kingdom. And by divine covenant, I refer to covenant between God and man. Inherent in any of these covenants is the concept of a lasting commitment to a clearly defined relationship.

HUMAN COVENANTS

Human covenants or covenants between human parties are often aimed at fostering a long-term commitment to a relationship. Entering into such a covenant is a declaration of trust in that relationship, as well as acceptance of its terms.

Depending on the nature of the personalities involved in the relationship, a human covenant is often given different names. For instance, when two people enter into a business partnership, they use a contract to define the partnership. When it is between countries, it is called a treaty; in a social setting, it means a lifelong friendship agreement; or it can refer to a marriage when it involves a man and a woman bound in holy matrimony.

The Scripture contains numerous examples of human covenants. When Abimelech and Isaac decided to settle their land dispute, they entered into a covenant to live in peace. (Genesis 26:26-31). Joshua and the Gibeonites bound themselves, by oath, to live in peace together (Joshua 9:15). Solomon and Hiram made a binding agreement to live and work in peace together (1 Kings 5:12). There was also the case of Jonathan and David making a covenant (1 Samuel 18:3) which essentially stipulated that, in return for Jonathan's kindness in informing David of his father's plans—making possible his escape—David, when he ascended the throne, would show mercy to Jonathan's descendants.

In 2 Chronicles 23:16, we find Jehoiada the priest making a covenant with the people and the king that they should be the Lord's people, which, in the light of what immediately follows obviously denotes that he agreed to grant them certain religious privileges in return for their undertaking to destroy the system of Baal worship.

A careful consideration of these human examples will help us understand and better appreciate the covenants which God has made with His children.

I need to emphasize here, that except for the covenant of marriage which involves God and thus more divine than physical in nature, most covenants made between humans are mainly for the purpose of seeking personal interests. This contrasts sharply with the covenant that God makes with us.

SATANIC COVENANTS

Satanic covenants are pacts made with the demonic kingdom, usually in exchange for a favor. These covenants are made sometimes knowingly but most times unknowingly – yet whatever the case is, they are usually very powerful in subjecting individuals, households and sometimes generations to a lifetime of perpetual slavery and destruction.

In cases where people knowingly enter into such covenants, it usually involves those who are desperate for instant success, fame, riches, fruit of the womb or advantage over rivals and competitors. This makes them to consult sorcerers, diviners and other people who are said to possess magical powers. In this case, the terms are clearly spelt out (of course, without the hidden repercussions and complications). The process often appears simple – "give this in return for that" – but the implications are usually very grave.

A typical example of the process of such covenants is contained in one of the temptations of Jesus Christ – which is a representation of what a typical human faces from day-to-day. Matthew 4:8-10 says,

> *"Again, the devil took Him up on an exceedingly high mountain, and showed Him all the kingdoms of the world and their glory. And he said to Him, "All these things I will give You if You will fall down and worship me." Then Jesus said to him, "Away with you, Satan! For it is written, You shall worship the Lord your God, and Him only you shall serve."*

What the devil intended here was to bring Christ under his dominion, through the pretext of rewarding Him with what already belongs to Him. And it is with the same seemingly harmless enticement that many, especially in the political, business and entertainment worlds today, are made to mortgage their souls to Satan. And since Satan cannot give an apple without hiding a worm in it, such people, except they are delivered by the power of God, often live their lives in secret anguish (despite the façade of fame and success that they project to the world) and die miserable deaths.

For those who unknowingly enter into covenants with the devil, it is often through carelessness or lack of discernment. To begin with, even the least consultation with anyone having "special powers" for help or fiddling with such items as horoscopes, Ouija boards and the likes are gateways to lasting covenants with the demonic kingdom. Sometimes watching certain movies, listening to certain songs, buying certain mementos and artifacts, engaging in sexual intimacy with certain individuals, joining certain associations and false churches, as well as partaking in certain feasts, are doorways to compact with the satanic world. And many have by this brought themselves under lasting yokes of the devil. This was why Paul warned the Corinthians,

> *"Observe Israel after the flesh: Are not those who eat of the sacrifices partakers of the altar? What am I saying then? That an idol is anything, or what is offered to idols is anything? Rather, that the things which the Gentiles sacrifice they sacrifice to demons and not to God, and I do not want you to have fellowship with demons. You cannot drink the cup of the Lord and the cup of demons; you cannot partake of the Lord's table and of the table of demons." (1 Corinthians 10:18-21).*

There are also those who engage in such activities as bathing in certain rivers known to have "magical powers" or taking themselves or their children through certain communal rituals. Many demonic yokes have been introduced into people's lives through this means and such individuals have to bear the burdens for as long as they live and may even transfer them to their children after them.

You may be wondering why I had to go to such elaborate length in discussing satanic covenants when this book is actually about divine covenants. Well, the purpose is to give you an insight into the power of covenants but, more importantly, to help you better appreciate the covenant that God makes with His children and why it is indeed true that Christ's yoke (His covenant terms) is easy and his burden is light (Matthew 11:28-30).

DIVINE COVENANT

A divine covenant, which is the grandest, purest and loveliest of all covenants, is an agreement between God and man - an agreement whose terms are set by God Himself. It is the ultimate demonstration of God's love for mankind because in this agreement, God binds Himself to bless, sustain, support and protect us in return for our commitment to serve Him and keep His commandments. So, in a divine covenant, God defines the basic obligations that He imposes on Himself and, usually, on the human party.

A man of God has rightly said that "A divine covenant can be compared to a sacred constitution established to regulate human relationships with God. It is a formal declaration of God's will and purpose. It typically expresses His deep love for humanity and reveals one or more major aspects of His plan for humanity's salvation."

Four distinctive and refreshing truths that we can glean from the description of a divine covenant are:

1. A divine covenant is unilateral (one way). Covenants between humans are often bilateral because they involve two or more equal parties who jointly agree

to bind themselves with an oath or some other means to engage in a deal that guarantees equal benefits and responsibilities for both parties. This is not the case in a divine covenant. A divine covenant does not involve two equal parties. In a divine covenant, God, in love, condescends to initiate the covenant, determines the conditions, stipulates special promises for adherence and keeps to His side of the bargain. Thus, in a divine covenant, persons are recipients, not contributors. They are called to accept it as offered, to keep it as demanded, and to receive the results that God, by oath, assures will not be withheld.

2. A divine covenant guarantees freedom, especially for the human party. Unlike both human and satanic covenants, God's terms are not grievous (1 John 5:3). Not only does He ask of us what we should do naturally but also makes it easy for us to comply.

3. There is a sure guarantee of compliance from God. Again, unlike human covenants where either party can fail, in divine covenant, God can never fail. Human parties in a covenant usually have to "sleep with one eye open", watching closely to ensure that the other party does not default. With God, however, there is absolutely nothing to fear (We shall see ample evidence of this in a later chapter).

There is usually a warning not to keep all of one's eggs in one basket. But there's absolute rest and comfort for all who keep their eggs in God's basket. He has never failed, He will never fail!

4. In both human and satanic covenants, each party jostles to outsmart the other and get the better bargain for themselves. With God, however, there is no competition or self-consideration. All He seeks is our benefit. He has all we need for life and godliness, for peace and comfort, for progress and prosperity, for protection and security. All He wants to do in inviting us into a covenant relationship is for Him to shower us with exclusive blessings that will distinguish us from others outside of His covenant. Through the substance of His covenants—His divine commitments—God binds Himself to perform all of the promises He makes. The undergirding principle of divine covenant is thus aptly summarized in Hosea 2:19-20,

"I will betroth you to Me forever; Yes, I will betroth you to Me In righteousness and justice, In lovingkindness and mercy; I will betroth you to Me in faithfulness, And you shall know the Lord."

I don't know what kind of relationship you currently have with the Almighty God, but I can tell you that if you have not entered into a covenant relationship with Him, then you are missing a lot. It is not enough to be religious or to be a church-goer. It is not enough to have a Christian name or even be a worker in the church. None of this brings us into that place of unrivalled glory, peace, joy, abundance, victory, dominion and fulfillment that God wants us to be; what they can do, at best, is get us stuck at the sideline of the manifold provisions that God has reserved for those who have entered into

Covenant Keeper, Not a Covenant Breaker

a thriving covenant relationship with Him. As it is written,

> *"Eye has not seen, nor ear heard, nor have entered into the heart of man the things which God has prepared for those who love Him" (1 Corinthians 2:9).*

What's more, as we shall see when we look at specific details and examples of divine covenants in the next chapter, divine covenants are usually accompanied with great and precious promises. In other words, scriptural promises are offshoots of divine covenants. These promises are all-encompassing for every need of mankind. They are rich, full, satisfying, assuring and life-changing. Above all, they are SURE!

CHAPTER 3

GOD, THE COVENANT MAKER

Apart from the general blessings that God bestows on the whole of humanity as the caring Father of all creation, He constantly longs for a special category of people upon whom He can exclusively demonstrate the fullness of His goodness; people whose lives can continually show forth His praise by reflecting His glory and beauty. It is for this reason that He often calls mankind into a covenant relationship with Him.

We find a reflection of this even among humankind. There is the general love that an individual bestows on fellow humans but there is the special love that one bestows on those to whom one is bonded in an intimate relationship. Moreover, since God does not deserve half-hearted commitment from any of His creatures, He seeks those who would fully acknowledge his ownership of their lives, so He can reveal Himself fully to them and bless them in uncommon ways. The avenue by which this distinction between the true worshippers of God and the nominal worshippers is achieved is establishment of a covenant relationship.

What this means therefore is that covenant is at the heart of God's dealings with mankind from the time of Adam and Eve till now. Take a look through the Scripture again and you will find that everything about the Bible, redemption from sin and indeed Christianity is about covenants. As Mark Jones wrote, "All true theology is based on some form of a divine covenant. The Christian religion must be understood covenantally, for that is how God has chosen to relate to man, whether in the garden or after the entrance of sin into the world."

What this means is that none who wants to have a meaningful relationship with God can actually avoid accepting the provisions of His covenants. The only way to diligently and fruitfully seek, understand and enjoy God is to enter into a covenant relationship with Him. Rightly has an author wrote: "God is a covenant-making and covenant-keeping God. If you have never thought of Him in these terms, then you have not yet begun to think about Him in the way he wants you to. God's Word describes those covenants, proclaiming Him to be a covenanting God. In a sense, the Bible is the book of His covenant. We even call it that – the Old and the New Covenants [Testaments]!"

THE BIBLE AS A BOOK OF COVENANTS

It is indeed absolutely apt to describe the Bible as a book of covenants. To begin with, the word "covenant" is found no fewer than twenty-five times in the very first book of the Bible; and it occurs again severally in the remaining books of the Pentateuch, in the Psalms and in the Prophets.

It is the same thing we find in the New Testament. When instituting the Lord's Supper, Jesus said,

"This cup is the new covenant in my blood "(Luke 22:20).

Also, when discussing the special blessings which God had conferred on the Israelites, Paul declared that to them belonged the covenants (Romans 9:4).

To the Galatians, he expounded the two covenants (Galatians 4:24-31). The Ephesian saints were also reminded that in their unregenerate days, they were strangers to the covenants of promise. The entire Epistle to the Hebrews is an exposition of the better covenant of which Christ is mediator (Hebrews 8:6).

Apart from the above revelations, it is absolutely true that we will find it absolutely enlightening and empowering if we consciously accept the Bible as a book of covenants. It is only through this understanding that we can get a full picture of the love and faithfulness of God throughout the generations of mankind, as well as the ultimate provision He has made for our general well-being.

Covenant Keeper, Not a Covenant Breaker

As Peter Gentry and Stephen Wellum have pointed out, covenants are the "backbone" of the storyline of the Bible. In other words, the Bible is not just a compilation of laws, moral principles, and stories. It has a definite and wonderful storyline that runs through all the books; it is the story of redemption, the story of God's boundless love and mercy to mankind, as well as the story of the preparation for His kingdom. This story progressively unfolds through the various covenants God made with his people, including you and me. Let's examine these covenants.

1. THE EDENIC COVENANT

The Edenic covenant refers to the covenant that God made with Adam (who was representing humanity as a whole) in the Garden of Eden. Here it is:

> *"And the Lord God commanded the man, saying, "Of every tree of the garden you may freely eat; but of the tree of the knowledge of good and evil you shall not eat, for in the day that you eat of it you shall surely die" (Genesis 2:16-17).*

It has always been the desire of God for man to have life and have it abundantly (John 10:10). So, in the passage above, we find God making a proposal to Adam that he would continue to enjoy life and all the divine provisions that had been made for him for as long as he stayed away from the tree of the knowledge of good and evil.

As has already been noted, God deserves and desires our absolute commitment, in return for all the glorious blessings He longs to shower upon us. It was for this same reason that He made the above proposition to Adam. There was no point in lavishing man with precious blessings if he felt that God was not deserving of unalloyed reverence and submission.

In the proposition of God to Adam therefore, we have all the elements of a covenant, namely: the contracting parties - the Lord God and man; an obligation to perform – not to eat of the forbidden tree; a penalty in case of disobedience; as well as reward for continued obedience.

As I hinted above, in the Edenic covenant, Adam acted not just for himself only, but as a representative of the whole of his posterity. In this capacity, Adam was a type of Christ, through whom God made the everlasting covenant, and who at the appointed time acted as the head and representative of His people: as it is written,

> *"over them that had not sinned after the similitude of Adam's transgression, who is the figure of him that was to come"* (Romans 5:14).

Unfortunately, Adam and Eve disobeyed and broke the terms of the Edenic covenant, and thus received the punishment of death, spiritually and physically. This punishment was equally passed on to all their offspring, and death continues to this day to be the wages of sin (Proverbs 10:16; Romans 6:23).

But, then, God in His infinite love and mercy, created what can be described as a second part to the Edenic covenant. This is often called the Covenant of

Redemption. As God was informing Adam and Eve about the curses their sin had brought them, He revealed an unconditional covenant with mankind in His curse upon the serpent when He said:

> *"And I will put enmity between you and the woman, and between your seed and her Seed; He shall bruise your head, and you shall bruise His heel" (Genesis 3:15).*

The word "Seed" here refers to Christ, while the serpent that deceived Adam and Eve represents Satan. God was, thus, through the second part of the Edenic covenant foretelling that Satan would have a minor victory upon Christ through the crucifixion, and therefore "strike his heel." But this damage would be temporary. In the end, Christ would rise and deliver a fatal blow to Satan and his kingdom, and the snake's head would be crushed (Romans 16:20).

2. THE NOAHIC COVENANT

Although less frequently talked about, this is one of the most interesting divine covenants recorded in the Scripture. This is not just because it illustrates the unfathomable loving-kindness of God to humanity but also because it provides us with one of the most tangible evidences of God's faithfulness to His words, as well as accurately explaining a natural phenomenon – the rainbow (there will be details of this in the next chapter).

While mankind awaited the arrival of the promised "Seed", God continued to provide avenues for man to be reconciled back to Him. This was what brought about the Noahic covenant. With the entrance of sin into the world, the offspring of Adam became incorrigibly decadent, sinking deeper and deeper into the abyss of rebellion against God. Genesis 6:5-6 says,

> *"Then the Lord saw that the wickedness of man was great in the earth, and that every intent of the thoughts of his heart was only evil continually. And the Lord was sorry that He had made man on the earth, and He was grieved in His heart."*

Yet, the faithfulness of God remained unaltered. He had made the earth to be inhabited by man (Isaiah 45:18); and even though He was to cut off corrupted humanity from the earth, He was bent on giving man a second chance. But even that was to be conditional. He instructed Noah, who alone had found favor in His sight, to construct an ark that would preserve as many as would enter into it from the impending destruction. You can compare this entering into the ark as entering into a covenant with God. I tell you, entering into a covenant with God guarantees maximum security from attacks, heartaches and destructions.

Sadly again, despite repeated pleading, the majority of mankind refused to accept God's offer of mercy. So, God told Noah,

> *"But I will establish My covenant with you; and you shall go into the ark—you, your sons, your wife, and your sons' wives with you. And of every living thing of all flesh you shall bring two of every sort into the ark, to keep them alive with you; they shall be male and female." (Genesis 6:18-19).*

Covenant Keeper, Not a Covenant Breaker

As I guess you already know, Noah obeyed and the flood came and destroyed all that was not in the ark. Thereafter, after the flood had abated and Noah had come out of the ark, he did something instructive – he offered a thanksgiving offering to God. However, even as he did that, he had a lot to worry about. First, it was true that he and his family had escaped the flood, but since they were imperfect humans, what guarantee was there that God would still not wipe them out by and by? Second, he had witnessed rain fall continuously for several days, leading to the extermination of all plant and animal life. Couldn't this still happen again? And then, there were the animals that he had taken into the ark. They certainly outnumbered his human family and could easily turn wild again and inflict untold harm on him and his people.

P. Fairbairn, describing the situation Noah was, wrote: "In one respect the world seemed to have suffered material loss by the visitation of the deluge. Along with the agents and instruments of evil there had also been swept away by it the emblems of grace and hope— paradise with its tree of life and its cherubim of glory. We can conceive Noah and his household, when they first left the ark, looking around with melancholy feelings on the position they now occupied, not only as being the sole survivors of a numerous offspring, but also as being themselves bereft of the sacred memorials which bore evidence of a happy past, and exhibited the pledge of a yet happier future. An important link of communion with Heaven, it might well have seemed, was broken by the change thus brought through the deluge on the world".

Praise be to the Almighty God, whose knowledge and compassion know no bounds. The time in which Noah offered the thanksgiving offering provided a good opportunity to address all of his unspoken concerns and allay his fears. God, as usual, did this by establishing a covenant with him and thus binding Himself to the fulfillment.

> "Then the Lord said in His heart, "I will never again curse the ground for man's sake, although the imagination of man's heart is evil from his youth; nor will I again destroy every living thing as I have done. "While the earth remains, Seedtime and harvest, Cold and heat, Winter and summer, And day and night Shall not cease."...So God blessed Noah and his sons, and said to them: "Be fruitful and multiply, and fill the earth. And the fear of you and the dread of you shall be on every beast of the earth, on every bird of the air, on all that move on the earth, and on all the fish of the sea. They are given into your hand. Every moving thing that lives shall be food for you. I have given you all things, even as the green herbs. But you shall not eat flesh with its life, that is, its blood... Then God spoke to Noah and to his sons with him, saying: "And as for Me, behold, I establish My covenant with you and with your descendants after you, and with every living creature that is with you: the birds, the cattle, and every beast of the earth with you, of all that go out of the ark, every beast of the earth. Thus I establish My covenant with you: Never again shall all flesh be cut off by the waters of the flood; never again shall there be a flood to destroy the earth." And God said: "This is the sign of

> *the covenant which I make between Me and you, and every living creature that is with you, for perpetual generations: I set My rainbow in the cloud, and it shall be for the sign of the covenant between Me and the earth. It shall be, when I bring a cloud over the earth, that the rainbow shall be seen in the cloud; and I will remember My covenant which is between Me and you and every living creature of all flesh; the waters shall never again become a flood to destroy all flesh." (Genesis 8:20-22; 9:1-15).*

God could certainly have made the above resolutions all by Himself without having to express anything to Noah; but in consistency with His nature of holiness, faithfulness and love in His dealings with mankind, He chose to bind Himself with a solemn oath so that the performance thereof may be plain for all to see.

Yet, just as it was at the time of Adam, mankind soon began to fall short of the terms of the covenant, beginning with Noah himself who got himself so drunk as to become naked; to Ham, who discovered his father's nakedness and made mockery of it, to the rest of humanity. The unfaithfulness of mankind, however, had no effect on the abiding faithfulness of God.

3. ABRAHAMIC COVENANT

The Abrahamic covenant was the covenant that God established with Abraham. And as we consider its details, I want you to pay particular attention, not just because it is again a powerful testament to God's faithfulness but because its provisions and blessings are for every believer in Christ today. As Galatians 3:29 says,

> *"And if you are Christ's, then you are Abraham's seed, and heirs according to the promise."*

The actual Abrahamic Covenant is found in Genesis 12:1–3:

> *"Now the Lord had said to Abram: "Get out of your country, From your family And from your father's house, To a land that I will show you. I will make you a great nation; I will bless you And make your name great; And you shall be a blessing. I will bless those who bless you, And I will curse him who curses you; And in you all the families of the earth shall be blessed."*

Abraham is a key figure in both world history and the history of redemption. His call out of Ur of the Chaldees was a turning point in the revelation of God's purposes of grace for mankind. In the above verses, we find God singling him out to bless him and to make him be a source of blessing to the world. This extends to all believers of all ages and nations who share his faith in God and Christ (Romans 4.12-17).

There are three main features of this covenant:

- The promise of land (Genesis 12:1). God called Abraham from Ur of the Chaldees to a land that He would give him (Genesis 12:1). This promise is reiterated in Genesis 13:14–18 where it is confirmed by a shoe covenant; its dimensions are given in Genesis 15:18–21.

- The promise of descendants (Genesis 12:2). God promised Abraham that He would make a great nation out of him. Abraham, who was 75 years old and childless (Genesis 12:4), was promised many descendants. This promise is amplified in Genesis 17:6 where God promised that nations and kings would descend from the aged patriarch.

- The promise of blessing and redemption (Genesis 12:3). God promised to bless Abraham and the families of the earth through him. This promise is amplified in the New Covenant (Hebrews 8:6–13) and has to do with "Israel's spiritual blessing and redemption."

Interestingly, the pledge made by God in the covenant is renewed several times in Scripture to Abraham's descendants through Isaac and Jacob. Beyond this however is a powerful reminder that God's covenants with us are simply for our good and He is ever committed to bringing them to pass, regardless of circumstances.

The ultimate purpose of the Abrahamic covenant was to make known the stock from which the Messiah was to spring. This was the most prominent aspect of truth revealed in it: the appearing of the promised Seed in Abraham's own line.

4. THE SINAITIC COVENANT

Just as God called Abraham to Himself, He equally extended the same hand of fellowship to his descendants – the Israelites – by calling them into a covenant relationship with Him. The terms of the covenant are codified into the Sinaitic (or more popularly called the

Mosaic) covenant.

The Sinaitic covenant therefore refers to the covenant that God made with the ancient Israelites at Mount Sinai, to give them His special blessings and protection on the condition that they obey His commandments. This covenant marked a memorable epoch in the history of the Israelites. It also marked the beginning of a new era in the history of the human race, being a momentous step in the series of divine dispensations toward fallen mankind.

Here is a vital lesson to learn – covenant is a personal affair and not a one-size-fits-all thing. God makes provision for each individual to come into a personal, thriving relationship with Him. As already stated, the Abrahamic covenant was renewed with Isaac and with Jacob. And it is the same extension that we find in the case of the Israelites.

The condition of the Sinaitic covenant is contained in Exodus 19:5:

> *"Now therefore, if you will indeed obey My voice and keep My covenant, then you shall be a special treasure to Me above all people; for all the earth is Mine. And you shall be to Me a kingdom of priests and a holy nation."*

What this reveals is that the primary purpose of the Sinaitic covenant was to serve as a codified fulfillment of the promises made to Abraham: to give him numerous offspring, to establish his offspring in the land of Canaan, to preserve pure the stock from which the Messiah was to spring, and to preserve them there until

Christ actually appeared in the flesh. Thus the Sinaitic dispensation had served its purpose by the time the Son of God manifested.

More importantly, God's ultimate design under the Sinaitic dispensation was to furnish a clear and full demonstration of the utter inability of fallen man, even under the most favorable conditions or circumstances, to meet His holy and righteous requirements; thereby making manifest the exceeding sinfulness of sin and the imperative need of an all-sufficient Savior.

5. THE NEW COVENANT

This is the grand covenant with which God achieves His ultimate program of redemption and reconciliation for humanity. It was to perfect all that the Sinaitic law could not achieve in our lives and to grant us full reconciliation with God and direct access to the throne of grace. All barriers and limitations to our being whom God originally designed us to be – a people of all-round dominion - is entirely removed. And it is no surprise that the token of the covenant is the blood of Jesus Christ that was shed on the cross for humanity.

Someone summarized the superiority of the New Covenant thus:

> *"To run and work the law commands,*
>
> *Yet gives me neither feet nor hands.*
>
> *But better news the gospel brings:*

It bids me fly, and gives me wings!"

Through the New Covenant that Christ established and the gift of the Holy Spirit who indwells all believers, we not only know what to do, we also have been given the power and strength to do it. Moreover, since all the previous covenants were pointing to this, anyone who enters into this covenant through the blood of Jesus Christ is not only empowered to live a life pleasing to God but also enjoys all the blessings and promises associated with all of the covenants in a higher dimension.

Most delightfully, with the New Covenant comes the promise of a personal relationship with God. For as many as fulfill the simple requirement of the covenant – believing and appropriating the redemptive work of Jesus on the cross – God clearly promises:

> *"They shall be My people, and I will be their God; then I will give them one heart and one way, that they may fear Me forever, for the good of them and their children after them" (Jeremiah 32:38-39).*

So, now, for as many of us as have entered into the new covenant with God through Jesus Christ, God isn't just God to us. He's not just there. He's not simply the omnipotent, Supreme Being who created all things and upholds all things. Rather, we rejoice that He is our God!

CHAPTER 4

GOD, THE COVENANT KEEPER

Great indeed is the faithfulness of the Lord our God. His declaration in Psalm 89:34 is ever true –

"My covenant I will not break, Nor alter the word that has gone out of My lips."

Testimonies and records from the beginning of time show that God is not just a covenant-making but a covenant-keeping God. No one who has ever struck a bargain with Him has ever had a cause to blame Him for defaulting. As John Fawcett once said, "Our fathers trusted in him, and were not confounded, they relied on his faithful word, and were delivered. All the succeeding generations of his people, from the beginning of time, have placed their confidence in what he has spoken, and none could ever charge him, either with lack of compassion, or breach of truth."

Covenant Keeper, Not a Covenant Breaker

Have you ever wondered why in many of the exhortations that God gave the Israelites through Moses He often reminded them of His past faithfulness and wonders in their lives? It was to assure them that faithfulness is the very essence of His character; and if He had never failed them before then they had no reason to ever doubt His commitment to any His promises and covenants.

REVISITING THE COVENANTS

So, as a proof of the immutable faithfulness of God, I want us to reconsider the same promises attached to the covenants that we examined in the last chapter and see their fulfilments for the purpose of consolidating our faith.

First is the Adamic covenant. As we have considered, even though man failed his side of the covenant, God's original purpose for creating mankind remains unchanged. On the physical side, the mandate and blessing that God bestowed on mankind to be fruitful, multiply, fill the earth and have dominion over it has remained constant.

Look how far humanity has come in dominating the earth! Unbelievable inventions and advancements have continued to be made in all the various fields of human endeavor. The earth, the seas and the skies have continued to be explored, exploited and domesticated for the benefits of mankind. Amazing medical, scientific and technological breakthroughs have been made; yet mankind remains unrelenting in their achievements.

On the spiritual side – which is the more important aspect – consider the infinitely glorious and irreversible victory that Jesus obtained on the cross over the devil and the great salvation He obtained for humanity. It took thousands of years for God's promise of the Seed of the woman bruising the head of the serpent to come to fulfillment; yet, it eventually did. Man's lost position and relationship with God in the Garden was restored. Many had waited for the promised deliverance and it seemed it might not happen, but God who never lies nor break His covenants ensured the fulfilment in the nick of time.

Of the glorious victory that Christ recorded on our behalf over Satan and the forces of hell, the Bible records:

> *"Having disarmed principalities and powers, He made a public spectacle of them, triumphing over them in it." (Colossians 2:15).*

Thus the powers that held men bound to the captivity of Satan, following the fall in the Garden, have been paralyzed totally and decisively. The chains of sin, afflictions, oppressions, diseases and limitations have been broken on the cross.

For as many as appropriate the victory of Calvary in their lives therefore, the head of the serpent is permanently bruised and his power will no longer hold sway in their lives.

> *"But He was wounded for our transgressions, He was bruised for our iniquities; The chastisement for our peace was upon Him, and by His stripes we are healed." (Isaiah 53:5).*

How about the Noahic covenant? I told you earlier on

that this remains one of the most significant of the covenants – especially with the beautiful and tangible proof of God's faithfulness that emanated from it. God promised Noah, in a bid to alleviate his fear, that NEVER again would He destroy the earth with a deluge. He also told him that while the earth remained, seedtime and harvest, and cold and heat, and summer and winter, and day and night shall not cease. And to demonstrate His commitment to His pledge, He gave Noah a concrete sign – the rainbow.

Indeed, if there's any reason why you should never doubt any promise of God, the rainbow remains a solid reference. Thousands of years have passed after God gave this assurance and yet till today, the rainbow continues to appear as a constant reminder of the oath that God has bound Himself with for our sakes. A minister of God has noted that: "These promises were made by God upward of four thousand years ago; and the unfailing fulfillment of them annually, all through the centuries, affords a striking demonstration of His faithfulness.

"Moreover, in their fulfillment we have exemplified a fact which is generally lost sight of by the world today; namely, that behind nature's "laws" is nature's Lord…A casual observance of nature's "laws" reveals the fact that they are not uniform in their operation; and therefore if we had not Scripture, we would be without any assurance that the seasons might not radically change and the whole earth again be inundated. Nature's "laws" did not prevent the Deluge in Noah's days. How then should they hinder a recurrence of it in ours? How blessed for the child of God to listen to this guarantee of his Father!"

Based on the Noahic covenant, we can rest assured that regardless of the intensity and ferocity of any rainfall, the sun will definitely shine again. No matter how scorching the sun may be, it will sooner or later give way to the rain of comfort. And it has continued to be so from century to century. What does this tell you child of God? What deluge of challenges are you currently facing and you think it's all over for you? In which way does it seem as if there is darkness all around you because of confusion and frustration? The assurance of God to you is that

> "Weeping may endure for a night, But joy comes in the morning." (Psalm 30:5).

And then we have the Abrahamic covenant - which is anchored on several promises, all of which came to fulfilment in the life of Abraham and his descendants and have continued to be manifested in the lives of believers who are his spiritual descendants.

First, God promised to make Abraham a great nation. God started to fulfill this promise when he gave Abraham and Sarah a son: Isaac. Interestingly, as at the time God gave the promise to Abraham, he and his wife were already old and, scientifically, unfit to produce children. In fact, when God told Abraham through the angels that he had entertained in his house, that they were going to have children, Sarah's immediate reaction was to laugh in disbelief because it all sounded so ridiculous (Genesis 18:12). Yet, God, with whom there is no impossibility or unfaithfulness, fulfilled His word and made the impossible possible. The nation of Israel is that great nation descended from Abraham, Isaac, and Jacob.

Second, God promised to bless Abraham with material blessings. And true to this promise, God abundantly blessed Abraham with prosperity. Genesis 13:2 says,

> *"Abram was very rich in livestock, in silver, and in gold"*

The testimony of Abraham's servant is even more reflective of God's faithfulness. He declared,

> *"The Lord has blessed my master greatly, and he has become great; and He has given him flocks and herds, silver and gold, male and female servants, and camels and donkeys." (Genesis 24:35).*

Abraham and Lot could not live in the same area because *"their possessions were so great" (Genesis 13:6).*

Third, God promised to make Abraham's name great. Again, God kept this promise to the letter. Abraham is the father of the faithful. The Israelites who are mainly Judaists refer to him as their father. Christians revere him as the father of faith. Throughout the Old and the New Testaments, his name continues to resonate in greatness.

Fourth, God promised to bless those who blessed Abraham and to curse those who cursed him. To begin with, all who were associated with Abraham were blessed. God blessed Lot with great possessions (Genesis 13) because of his association with Abraham. Even Ishmael who was an illegitimate son was blessed abundantly for Abraham's sake. God cursed Pharaoh for taking Abraham's wife into his harem (Genesis 12). God also plagued Abimelech's household for a similar wrong.

Moreover, throughout history nations that have blessed Israel have experienced God's blessing. On the other hand, nations that have cursed Israel and the Jews have experienced God's judgments in diverse ways.

Fifth, God promised to bless all the families of the earth in Abraham. This promise of universal blessing finds its fulfillment in Jesus Christ, the Seed of Abraham (Galatians 3:16). This was why the angels proclaimed at Christ's birth: *"Glory to God in the highest, and on earth peace, goodwill toward men!"*

Aside from the above, God made every one of His promises to Abraham good, even years after Abraham's death. For instance, while God told Abraham that his descendants would be enslaved by another nation, he promised that they would be delivered after 400 years in captivity. And, true to the promise, years after Abraham had died and many Israelites had even forgotten than God gave such a promise, God fulfilled His promise and brought the people out of their captivity with a mighty hand.

King David, the Psalmist, documented God's goodness to Israel as a result of the covenant with Abraham thus:

> "He brought them forth also with silver and gold: and there was not one feeble person among their tribes. Egypt was glad when they departed: for the fear of them fell upon them. He spread a cloud for a covering; and fire to give light in the night. The people asked, and he brought quails, and satisfied them with the bread of heaven. He opened the rock, and the waters gushed out; they ran in the dry places like a river. FOR HE REMEMBERED HIS HOLY PROMISE, AND ABRAHAM HIS SERVANT. And he brought forth his people with joy, and his chosen with gladness: And gave them the lands of the heathen: and they inherited the labor of the people; That they might observe his statutes, and keep his laws. Praise ye the Lord." (Psalm 105:37-45).

Did you notice the highlighted portion? God remembered, hundreds of years after the promise had been made and the initial recipient had died. Indeed, the continued survival and prosperity of the nation of Israel today is primarily because of that age-old covenant. You can't fault this God! As for the Mosaic covenant and the numerous promises that were made to the Israelites in it, there are overflowing evidences of God keeping His side of the covenant, despite repeated violations by the Israelites. In fact, looking at the continued longsuffering of God in the face of Israel's constant rebellion, someone wrote: "Nothing is more remarkable than the grace of God, and nothing illustrates that grace more than God's perseverance and goodness to a continually rebellious and impatient people."

The Psalmist again testified to this:

"For their heart was not steadfast with Him, Nor were they faithful in His covenant. But He, being full of compassion, forgave their iniquity, And did not destroy them. Yes, many a time He turned His anger away, And did not stir up all His wrath; For He remembered that they were but flesh, A breath that passes away and does not come again." (Psalm 78:37-39).

In truth, the catalogue of God's faithfulness to the Israelites is simply mind-boggling and too numerous to enumerate. I already pointed out in the opening chapter how God ensured that no enchantment or divination could prevail against them. And it is a testament to God's faithfulness that the reason that Balak sent for Balaam to stop the Israelites was because God had so elevated them that they had become unstoppable in might and conquest. They had, in accordance with God's promise, been set on high above all other nations. He fed them with angel's food and did many unprecedented wonders among them.

So much was the glory of God upon them that their fame spread far and wide ahead of them. Balak testified to this when He said,

"Now this company will lick up everything around us, as an ox licks up the grass of the field." (Numbers 22:4).

It was the same testimony that the people of Jericho gave about the Israelites. As Rahab told the spies that Joshua sent,

"For we have heard how the Lord dried up the water of the Red Sea for you when you came out of Egypt, and what you

> *did to the two kings of the Amorites who were on the other side of the Jordan, Sihon and Og, whom you utterly destroyed. And as soon as we heard these things, our hearts melted; neither did there remain any more courage in anyone because of you, for the Lord your God, He is God in heaven above and on earth beneath." (Joshua 2:10-11).*

But perhaps the greatest testimony of God's unfailing faithfulness to the covenant he established with the Israelites is the declaration of God Himself concerning the Israelites after their many years of persistently breaking His covenant. You would think He would cast them off forever or destroy them altogether. Yet, He just could not be compelled to renege on His covenant with them or their forefathers. He declared in Hosea 11:8-9,

> *"How can I give you up, Ephraim? How can I hand you over, Israel? How can I make you like Admah? How can I set you like Zeboiim? My heart churns within Me; My sympathy is stirred. I will not execute the fierceness of My anger; I will not again destroy Ephraim. For I am God, and not man..."*

Concerning the New Covenant in which God promised to freely forgive and redeem all who believe in Jesus from the guilt and power of sin, as well as giving them the power to love and serve Him from the heart, we have many testimonies in the Scripture concerning the fulfilment. Romans 8:3-4 testifies, "For what the law could not do in that it was weak through the flesh, God did by sending His own Son in the likeness of sinful flesh, on account of sin: He condemned sin in the flesh, that the righteous requirement of the law might be fulfilled in us who do not walk according to the flesh but according to the Spirit."

Titus 2:11 equally says, "For the grace of God that brings salvation has appeared to all men, teaching us that, denying ungodliness and worldly lusts, we should live soberly, righteously, and godly in the present age."

FURTHER TESTIMONIES OF HIS FAITHFULNESS

Away from the covenants that we have considered, several other proofs of God's faithfulness to His promises abound in the Scripture. Moses once testified,

> *"Therefore know that the Lord your God, He is God, the faithful God who keeps covenant and mercy for a thousand generations with those who love Him and keep His commandments" (Deuteronomy 7:9).*

Solomon too declared before all Israel,

> *"Blessed be the Lord, who has given rest to His people Israel, according to all that He promised. There has not failed one word of all His good promise, which He promised through His servant Moses." (1 Kings 8:56).*

Isaiah the Prophet also testified,

> *"LORD, you are my God; I will exalt you and praise your name, for in perfect faithfulness you have done wonderful things, things planned long ago" (Isaiah 25:1, NIV).*

But it is not only Bible saints who could attest to God's faithfulness; many contemporary believers have also seized every opportunity they have to recount the goodness of God in relation to His covenant promises. The renowned preacher, Charles Spurgeon, declared from his personal experience: "There is no more blessed way of living, than the life of faith based upon a covenant-keeping God; to know that we have no care, for He cares for us; that we need have no fear, except to fear Him; that we need have no troubles, because we have cast our burdens upon the Lord, and are confident that He will sustain us."

Missionary statesman, Hudson Taylor, wrote in one of his journal entries: "Our heavenly Father is a very experienced One. He knows very well that His children wake up with a good appetite every morning...He sustained three million Israelites in the wilderness for 40 years. We do not expect He will send three million missionaries to China; but if He did, He would have ample means to sustain them all...Depend on it, God's work done in God's way will never lack God's supply."

So also did Thomas Chisholm, author of the popular hymn, "Great is thy Faithfulness". Towards the end of his life, he wrote: "My income has not been large at any time due to impaired health in the earlier years which has followed me on until now. Although I must not fail to record here the unfailing faithfulness of a covenant-keeping God and that He has given me many wonderful displays of His providing care, for which I am filled with astonishing gratefulness."

With this mammoth cloud of witnesses, what other proofs do we need to be assured that God will not fail in any of His promises to us? He has not failed in the past and He will not fail in the present or in the future. Let this blessed assurance rouse you to cheerful hope, faith and expectations, dear believer. The Lord has promised that He will never leave you nor forsake you. He has promised to help you and keep you through the fire and the flood of life. This is all you need to rest in His faithfulness.

Learn from John Henry Jowett, who said: "Such a divine assurance ought to make me perfectly quiet in spirit. Restlessness in a Christian always spells disloyalty. The uncertainty is born of suspicion. There is a rift in the faith, and the disturbing breath of the devil blows through, and destroys my peace. If I am sure of my great Ally, my heart will not be troubled, neither will it be afraid…If the mighty Ally will never fail, I should never be afraid of the marshalled hosts of wickedness. "One with God is in a majority." "He always wins who sides with God." "The Lord is on my side, whom shall I fear?"

CHAPTER 5

KEEPING YOUR SIDE OF THE BARGAIN

Yes, you have a part to play in activating your covenant blessings. And it is of great importance that we consider this critical issue because we are living in a time when lots of misconception persist about the believer's responsibility under the New Covenant ratified by the blood of Jesus Christ. This indeed is a time of grace, which is totally different from the time of the Mosaic Law. Unlike the Mosaic period when people had to struggle to keep the commandments in order to receive the blessings of the covenant, Christ has become our Mediator and it is by the mercy we obtain from His sacrificial death that we receive unlimited access to the blessings of the New Covenant.

Sadly, many churchgoers have misunderstood this dispensation of grace to be a time when believers have no role to play in activating covenant blessings upon themselves. This has become a major emphasis in many congregations today. The blessings of the New Covenant, they claim, are unconditional, meaning that it does not depend on what we do or do not do. Or to put it more bluntly, our attitude to God and His word doesn't really matter, since Christ has already paid the price for all our transgressions in advance. And so people do whatever they like and treat God's word as they wish, while expecting the outpouring of His blessings. They want the goodies of the covenant but don't want any of its duties.

Let me quickly say this. First, while it is true that we live in the dispensation of grace, it does not mean that God has changed – He remains a holy God who cherishes holiness and righteousness. As a foremost minister of the gospel has written, "This brings before us a most important principle in the ways of God, which has often been lost sight of by men who only stress one side of the truth. That principle is that divine grace never sets aside the requirements of divine righteousness. God never shows mercy at the expense of His holiness…God is "light" as well as "love," and each of these divine perfections is exemplified in all His dealings with His people. Moreover, in the exercise of His sovereignty God never enforces the responsibility of the creature; and unless we keep both of these steadily in view, we not only become lopsided, but lapse into real error. The grace of God must not be magnified to the beclouding of His righteousness, nor His sovereignty pressed to the exclusion of human accountability."

Secondly, while we live in the dispensation of grace, the purpose of grace is not to make us to flagrantly disregard God's word – as Paul asked, "Shall we continue in sin that grace may abound?" Rather, the essence of grace is to make it easy for us to do the will of God in obedience and absolute submission. Titus 2:11-12 tells us the purpose of grace:

> *"For the grace of God that brings salvation has appeared to all men, teaching us that, denying ungodliness and worldly lusts, we should live soberly, righteously, and godly in the present age."*

Again, on the issue of requirements, the Bible makes it categorically clear that even in the New Testament, we certainly have to back our faith with works, that is, with responsibility. Paul wrote to the Corinthians,

> *"Therefore, having these promises, beloved, let us cleanse ourselves from all filthiness of the flesh and spirit, perfecting holiness in the fear of God." (2 Corinthians 7:1).*

He wrote to the Hebrews,

> *"Therefore we also, since we are surrounded by so great a cloud of witnesses, let us lay aside every weight, and the sin which so easily ensnares us, and let us run with endurance the race that is set before us"* (Hebrews 12:1).

Both of these verses and many others like them are from the New Testament and written under the dispensation of grace. This effectively nullifies the claim that we have no responsibility as believers under the New Covenant. Besides, I find it particularly interesting that while many believers claim that we have nothing to do with the Old Testament anymore, they are quick to delve into the same part of the Bible to dig up juicy promises and constantly confess that they are theirs to enjoy. Take, for instance, Deuteronomy 28. It contains many great promises of prosperity, abundant success and all-round victory which many of us like to claim. But the chapter begins with the requirement for enjoying these blessings. We cannot ignore this or simply close our eyes to it and jump into the blessing aspect. We must be sincere with the word of God if we must enjoy its riches.

INHERENT MESSAGE

I have devoted time to the above explanation so that we will not be delaying the fulfillment of our covenant blessings while thinking the fault is from God. Many believers are suffering needlessly today and many are not enjoying the blessings of the Kingdom – and they are thinking that it is probably because God has become unfaithful. Let me repeat: God can never be unfaithful and none of His promises can fail. The challenge rather comes from the wrong notions we have harbored about the dispensation of grace.

Jeremiah once asked,

> "Is there no balm in Gilead, Is there no physician there? Why then is there no recovery for the health of the daughter of my people?" (Jeremiah 8:22).

Of course there was still balm in Gilead but the people had rendered it ineffective in their lives through their wrong attitudes. God is the God of both the Old and the New Covenants and all His promises for us are unchanging. We are the ones to look whether we are keeping our side of the bargain or not.

Before I show you what the Lord specifically expects of us, let me further buttress on the point I made above with an example from the Corinthian Church, which reflects the case with many churches and believers today. The Corinthian church was a quintessential "charismatic" church. They believed so much in the freedom that comes with grace, as well as the manifestation of power and gifts that come with the Spirit's baptism. But like many New Testament believers, they assumed that nothing was required of them to enjoy covenant blessings. Thus they lived as they liked. And of course they suffered dire consequences that contradicted the blessings that should be the portion of God's children.

One of such areas in which the Corinthians violated God's requirements and attracted the attendant repercussions upon themselves, was in the Lord's Supper. Here is what Paul told them:

> *"Therefore when you come together in one place, it is not to eat the Lord's Supper. For in eating, each one takes his own supper ahead of others; and one is hungry and another is drunk. What! Do you not have houses to eat and drink in? Or do you despise the church of God and shame those who have nothing? What shall I say to you? Shall I praise you in this? I do not praise you… But let a man examine himself, and so let him eat of the bread and drink of the cup. For he who eats and drinks in an unworthy manner*

eats and drinks judgment to himself, not discerning the Lord's body. For this reason many are weak and sick among you, and many sleep." (1 Corinthians 11:20-30).

I want you to pay special attention to the last verse and observe a disturbing irony. How can it be that in a church where there was abundant manifestation of the gifts of the Spirit, members should be suffering from chronic illnesses, with some dying prematurely? Well, perhaps before Paul enlightened them, many would have thought that God was not being faithful to His promises of good health and long life for His children. And it is the same accusation that many are making against God today.

So, what are we expected to do to enjoy covenant blessings, even as New Testament believers?

BE IN A REAL COVENANT RELATIONSHIP WITH GOD

Romans 2:28-29 says,

> *"For he is not a Jew who is one outwardly, nor is circumcision that which is outward in the flesh; but he is a Jew who is one inwardly; and circumcision is that of the heart, in the Spirit, not in the letter…"*

I have mentioned before, with ample allusions, that our God is a God of covenants. That is the way He chooses to relate with those who would be His in truth. For the New Testament believer, the token of our covenant with God is redemption through the blood of Jesus. Without this, nothing else counts. Frequent church attendance, being a church worker or participating in some other religious roles does not translate to being in a covenant relationship with God. Only those who have had a definite encounter with Christ and have been washed in His blood are recognized as children of God.

> *"Nevertheless the solid foundation of God stands, having this seal: "The Lord knows those who are His," and, "Let everyone who names the name of Christ depart from iniquity." (2 Timothy 2:19).*

OBEY HIM IN ALL THINGS

> *"If you are willing and obedient, You shall eat the good of the land." (Isaiah 1:19).*

Don't be deceived – obedience to God's word is still a very much important secret to enjoying and keeping His blessings, even in this time of grace. In fact, now that grace is available is the very time we should be more obedient because the divine empowerment to do so has been given to us. The law that was abolished by the coming of Christ refers to the body of ceremonial rules that governed the daily lives of the Jewish people; it is not the body of moral laws. This is why you will find that even in the New Testament there are verses that echo contents of the moral laws given to the Israelites. For instance, in his letter to the Colossians, Paul wrote:

> *"Therefore put to death your members which are on the earth: fornication, uncleanness, passion, evil desire, and covetousness, which is idolatry. Because of these things the wrath of God*

> *is coming upon the sons of disobedience, in which you yourselves once walked when you lived in them. But now you yourselves are to put off all these: anger, wrath, malice, blasphemy, filthy language out of your mouth. Do not lie to one another, since you have put off the old man with his deeds"* (Colossians 3:5-9).

Aside from this general obedience to the word of God as described above, there is also individual obedience which involves paying careful attention to special or specific instructions given to us either directly through the word or Spirit of God, or through true messengers of God. This is why Jesus' mother told the servants at the wedding in Cana in Galilee – "Whatever He says to you, do it."

There are times when some instructions or prophetic declaration may sound ridiculous, but it is in our own interest that we obey. As Dr. B.J. Miller once said, "It is a great deal easier to do that which God gives us to do, no matter how hard it is, than to face the responsibilities of not doing it."

MAINTAIN ABSOLUTE FAITH IN HIS LEADING

This is the fulcrum on which other covenant blessing requirements rest. Hebrews 11:6 says,

> *"But without faith it is impossible to please Him, for he who comes to God must believe that He is, and that He is a rewarder of those who diligently seek Him."*

Without faith, we cannot trust God enough to enter into a lifelong covenant relationship with Him; nor can we fully obey His leading for our lives all the time, knowing that He can never mislead us.

What do you think made Abraham to leave His kindred to an unknown land which he and his descendants would forever inherit? What do you think made him to obey God again when He told him to sacrifice the only child he had managed to have in his old age? Of course he gave the answer to this himself when his son asked him where the lamb for the sacrifice was and he replied that God would provide (Genesis 22:28).

Why do you think Isaac, in obedience to God, remained in a land being ravaged by famine and even went ahead to sow in the same land? Why did Joseph refuse to yield to the enticements of Potiphar's wife? Why did Moses choose not to enjoy the riches of Pharaoh's household but chose rather to identify with the people of God? Why did Rahab hide the Israelites spies that were sent to herald the destruction of her city, Jericho? Why did the three Hebrew children not bow to the image erected by King Nebuchadnezzar? Why did the disciples abandon their businesses and vocations to follow Jesus Christ? It was FAITH in God and His word. They were confident that God would not default in His word. And nothing moves God into working in our favour and fighting our battles more than this.

No wonder the Bible says that it was by faith that the elders obtained a good report (Hebrews 11:2). But it was not only a good report that they obtained; they also enjoyed immeasurable covenant blessings and did extraordinary exploits. As Hebrews 11 again says,

> *"And what more shall I say? For the time would fail me to tell of Gideon and Barak and Samson and Jephthah, also of David and Samuel and the prophets: who through faith subdued kingdoms, worked righteousness, obtained promises, stopped the mouths of lions, quenched the violence of fire, escaped the edge of the sword, out of weakness were made strong, became valiant in battle, turned to flight the armies of the aliens" (32-34).*

The above are the three basic terms of enjoying the blessings of divine covenants. And I'm sure that, looking at these terms, you would agree that God's requirements are indeed not grievous. If you can take these simple steps, you can be sure that God will never disappoint you. He will be to you an ever present help in the troubles and triumphs of life. However, there is still one very important thing you need to know...

CHAPTER 6

TIMING IS KEY

Many people who knew the great New England preacher, Phillips Brooks, knew him for his quiet and gentle manners. Being human however, there were times when he suffered moments of frustration and despair. One day, a friend saw him feverishly pacing the floor like a caged lion. "What's the trouble, Mr. Brooks?" the friend asked. "The trouble is that I'm in a hurry, but God isn't!" the preacher replied.

Let's face it. There are times when we all find ourselves in the same situation as Mr. Brooks. However, there is a great kernel of truth in the preacher's response that we must pay particular attention to, especially as covenant children of God, eagerly expecting the fulfillment of His promises in our lives. Hebrews 10:36 says,

> "For ye have need of patience, that, after ye have done the will of God, ye might receive the promise" (KJV).

Yes, it is true that we may have fulfilled the basic terms of the covenant blessings in our lives; but we still have to know that the ultimate decision on the timing of the fulfillment of our expected visitation lies solely with God. This is what many do not understand, making them to get easily frustrated when promises and prophecies concerning their lives seem to delay, according to their own timing. And of course, with frustration come wrong attitudes and sometimes destructive choices.

T.D Jakes, in one of his writings says, "People who don't understand God's timing can become spiritually spastic, trying to make the right things happen at the wrong time. They don't get His rhythm – and everyone can tell they are out of step. They birth things prematurely, threatening the very lives of their God-given dreams."

So, we need to know, first of all, that God's timing and our timing may not always be the same. As the scripture states,

> "But, beloved, do not forget this one thing, that with the Lord one day is as a thousand years, and a thousand years as one day" (2 Peter 3:8).

Moreover, as we noted earlier, there are no accidents or emergencies with God. Known unto Him are all His works from the beginning. He has His timing for every purpose or event that He orchestrates, and this includes His promises for our lives. One thing you can be sure of, however, is that God's decisions are founded on wisdom, His ways are perfect and His timing is ALWAYS right. This is why Charles Spurgeon once exhorted, "If the Lord Jehovah makes us wait, let us do so with our whole hearts; for blessed are all they that wait for Him. He is worth waiting for. The waiting itself is beneficial to us: it tries faith, exercises patience, trains submission, and endears the blessing when it comes. The Lord's people have always been a waiting people."

We must learn to wait patiently,

> *"for the vision is for an appointed time" (Habakkuk 2:2).*

True to the words of Spurgeon above, God's notable people have always been waiting people. Search through the scriptures and you will find that all of the great heroes and heroines of faith who obtained promises also had to wait. James 5:10 states, "My brethren, take the prophets, who spoke in the name of the Lord, as an example of suffering and patience." We know that the Scripture is true about this. Abraham had to wait before obtaining the promised child. Noah had to wait for the flood to recede from the earth before he could leave the ark to resume normal life. The Israelites had to wait before their deliverance from Pharaoh's captivity came. Joseph had to wait before his dream could come true. David had to wait, several years after being anointed, before he could ascend the throne. And of Job in particular, the Scripture says,

> *"…Ye have heard of the patience of Job, and have seen the end of the Lord; that the Lord is very pitiful, and of tender mercy" (James 5:11, KJV).*

However, one thing common to all of these cases is that none of the people considered God's intervention as being too late, because God is never late, regardless of what we feel about our situations.

Another point I must emphasize here is that the period of waiting on God is not a time that God deliberately designed to punish us or to pretend that He doesn't feel our pain or see what we are going through. Rather, it is a time of preparing us to receive the best that He has for us. James 1:3-4 says, "Knowing that the testing of your faith produces patience. But let patience have its perfect work, that you may be perfect and complete, lacking nothing."

Many believers who have had to go through the experience of waiting and succeeded in allowing patience to have her perfect work in their lives can readily testify that it is one of the periods that God's faithfulness and loving-kindness are most demonstrated. Betsy Childs Howard, in her book, "Seasons of Waiting: Walking by Faith When Dreams Are Delayed" writes, "God doesn't waste our waiting. He uses it to conform us to the image of his Son." George Macdonald, writing from his own experience, notes: "He may delay because it would not be safe to give us at once what we ask: we are not ready for it. To give ere we could truly receive, would be to destroy the very heart and hope of prayer, to cease to be our Father. The delay itself may work to bring us nearer to our help, to increase the desire, perfect the prayer, and ripen the receptive condition." John Ortberg simply adds, "Biblically, waiting is not just something we have to do until we get what we want. Waiting is part of the process of becoming what God wants us to be."

WAITING THAT WORKS

In the book, "Waiting on God: What to Do When God Does Nothing", Wayne Stiles says, "Waiting is a very active part of living. Waiting on God, if we do it correctly, is anything but passive. Waiting works its way out in very deliberate actions, very intentionally searching the Scriptures and praying, intense moments of humility, and self-realization of our finiteness. With the waiting comes learning. I can't think of much I've learned that's positive from the times I've plowed ahead without waiting on God."

What I want you to observe is the opening of the second sentence – "Waiting on God, if we do it correctly…" This means that waiting is not something we do helplessly or haphazardly; it is something we do purposefully and productively. The waiting period is a time to renew strength, faith, courage and commitment. It is a time to MOUNT UP with wings as an eagle. Here is how:

MAINTAIN A POSITIVE ATTITUDE

The kind of waiting that works wonders is such that refuses to be caged, confined or crippled by challenges. It is not the kind of waiting that wears the signboard, "Look at me, I'm a miserable person." It is not the type that thrives on self-pity or craves sympathy from people around. Nor is it the type of waiting that transfers aggression to others or jealous of their progress. It is such that is fully anchored on trust in God's unfailing goodness, wisdom and ability. It is such waiting that rejoices in hope and constantly magnifies the God of the awaited blessing more than the blessing itself.

Andrew Murray, in his book, "Waiting on God", says it well: "The giver is more than the gift; God is more than the blessing. And our being kept waiting on Him is the only way for our learning to find our life and joy in Himself. Oh, if God's children only knew what a glorious God they have, and what a privilege it is to be linked in fellowship with Him, then they would rejoice in Him! Even when He keeps them waiting, they will learn to understand better than ever…His waiting will be the highest proof of His graciousness."

It is this kind of attitude that the three Hebrew children demonstrated. Despite the threats of Nebuchadnezzar and the intensity of the fiery furnace, they maintained a positive attitude, not particularly because they knew they would be delivered but because God Himself had become their joy and song, and His joy had become their strength! Thus, they declared, "O Nebuchadnezzar, we have no need to answer you in this matter. If that is the case, our God whom we serve is able to deliver us from the burning fiery furnace, and He will deliver us from your hand, O king. But if not, let it be known to you, O king, that we do not serve your gods, nor will we worship the gold image which you have set up" (Daniel 3:16-18). Of course, God was moved by their disposition and He rose swiftly to deliver them.

One effective way to maintain a positive attitude while waiting for your breakthrough is to constantly recall

God's goodness and faithfulness in the past. This will keep your heart from sinking in despair. As Charles Spurgeon once said of himself, "I know of nothing which so stimulates my faith in my Heavenly Father as to look back and reflect on His faithfulness to me in every crisis and every chilling circumstance of life. Over and over He has proved His care and concern for my welfare. Again and again I have been conscious of the Good Shepherd's guidance through dark days and deep valleys."

DECLARE POSITIVELY

This truth can never be over-emphasized – there is power to kill and power to quicken in the tongue. And even though God is a covenant-keeping God, the misuse of the tongue through negative declarations can thwart the release of His blessings upon our lives. Note that the unfaithfulness of man cannot nullify the faithfulness of God. But even after God must have granted, in the spiritual realm, that which He has promised, we can use our tongue to abort the manifestation.

The case of the Israelites reveals to us how this works. True to God's faithfulness, the land which He promised them was sighted by the spies and discovered to be truly overflowing with "milk and honey" – just as God had said. Sadly, however, majority of the people could not enter the land because of their declarations. God instructed Moses,

> *"Say to them, 'As I live,' says the Lord, 'just as you have spoken in My hearing, so I will do to you: The carcasses of*

> *you who have complained against Me shall fall in this wilderness, all of you who were numbered, according to your entire number, from twenty years old and above."* (Numbers 14:28-29).

In order not to fall into the same error, therefore, resolve to speak words of grace, life and peace over your life and situations. Recite the promises of God often over your life. Say what God says concerning you, not what men or circumstances are saying. This will keep the fiery darts of doubts and despair away from you. Learn from Job, who, in the midst of a most traumatic and devastating affliction, declared,

> *"…All the days of my appointed time will I wait, till my change come"* (Job 14:14, KJV); and *"For I know that my Redeemer lives…"* (Job 19:25).

REFUSE TO COMPROMISE

The time of waiting on God is usually a time of unprecedented barrage of pressure – pressure from within and without; pressure from the natural human frailty, pressure from Satan and his agents, and pressure from so-called well-wishers, most of which is often directed at making us compromise, take shortcuts, forsake God or generally try to outrun Him. The ultimate purpose of such pressure, of course, is to make us miss out on God's purpose and blessings for our lives.

What made Saul to lose God's favor and miss out on the divine purpose for his kingship was his repeated surrender to pressure to go against God's instruction.

In one instance, when Samuel asked him why he had disobeyed, he answered,

> *"Because I saw that the people were scattered from me..."* (1 Samuel 13:11).

At another time when Samuel asked him why he had spared Agag, king of Amalek, as well as the best of the city's livestock – contrary to God's express instruction – he replied,

> *"for the people spared the best of the sheep and the oxen, to sacrifice to the Lord your God"* (1 Samuel 15:15).

But God would have none of such excuses. Saul was immediately rejected and replaced. I pray that no one will take your rightful destiny.

But then, it was not only Saul who had to face pressure to compromise while waiting on God. Several other people were pressured and their responses had significant repercussions. Abraham gave in to pressure from his wife to have an affair with Hagar, her maid, while they awaited the promised child. Well, from that time till now, the battle between the offspring of Sarah and those of the bondwoman continues to reverberate around the world.

Joseph had the opportunity to seek a shortcut to end his miseries through the illicit pressure from Potiphar's wife. But thank God that he refused to compromise his faith. If he hadn't, he might never have gone to prison at that time – a time in which God had purposed for him to meet his destiny-helper: Pharaoh's butler.

Aaron, while deputizing for Moses and waiting for His return, succumbed to the pressure of the Israelites to make a god for them. The consequence was expectedly catastrophic for everyone. David, while waiting for his ascension to the throne, was pressured many times to kill Saul, so as to hasten his ascension. Again, like Joseph, he refused to yield and God rewarded him in due season. I don't know what pressure you are facing or the source of it; but my advice is,

> *"Wait on the Lord; Be of good courage, And He shall strengthen your heart; Wait, I say, on the Lord!" (Psalm 27:14).*

PRAY WITHOUT CEASING

It is for our own benefit that God enjoins us to pray without ceasing (1 Thessalonians 5:17). Among other reasons is the fact that it is not only God who is interested in our affairs; Satan and the host of hell too are very much interested – howbeit, in a destructive way. What this means is that it is possible that God fulfills His promises to us by answering our prayers, but if we are not vigilant in prayers, the enemy may come around to truncate the manifestation. This is why Jesus says that

> *"Men ought always to pray and not to faint." (Luke 18:1).*

And He demonstrated this Himself by living a life of prayer.

You may not understand how much the enemy contends with God's will for the believer's blessings and destiny until you explore the Scriptures. Paul, as mighty a minister as He was, told the Corinthians,

> *"For a great door and effectual is opened unto me, and there are many adversaries." (1 Corinthians 16:9).*

Who opened the great and effectual door for him? God. At another time, he wrote to the Thessalonians,

> *"Therefore we wanted to come to you—even I, Paul, time and again—but Satan hindered us" (1 Thessalonians 2:18).*

No wonder, He had to exhort the Ephesians (as well as you and me):

> *"Finally, my brethren, be strong in the Lord and in the power of His might. Put on the whole armor of God, that you may be able to stand against the wiles of the devil. For we do not wrestle against flesh and blood, but against principalities, against powers, against the rulers of the darkness of this age, against spiritual hosts of wickedness in the heavenly places" (Ephesians 6:10-13).*

We also know of the experience of Daniel whose prayer God faithfully answered but which the powers of the air fiercely contended against. Thank God that Daniel did not prematurely give up praying. And then we have the very proverb in Isaiah 37:3,

> *"...For the children have come to birth, but there is no strength to bring them forth."*

Most times, when the answers to our prayers and expectations are ready to manifest from the spiritual realm to the physical, only by effectual fervent prayer

Covenant Keeper, Not a Covenant Breaker

can we bring them forth. So, we must pray and keep praying, till the will of God is perfected in our lives.

Let me remind you again that our God is ever faithful. Generations of believers have placed their trust in Him and found Him to be a covenant-keeping God. All His promises are reliable and enduring. All you need do is enter a covenant relationship with Him and let Him be the Lord of your life and affairs. Place your confidence firmly in him and reject every suggestion of the enemy. In the nick of time, the Lord will visit you and your testimony like that of the Psalmist will be:

> *"When the Lord brought back the captivity of Zion, We were like those who dream. Then our mouth was filled with laughter, And our tongue with singing. Then they said among the nations, "The Lord has done great things for them." The Lord has done great things for us, And we are glad." (Psalm 126:1-3).*

CHAPTER 7

COVENANT PROMISES FOR EVERY SITUATION

Below are some precious promises that God has given us to enjoy. Pray and declare them in faith – and constantly look out for the manifestations in your life. God is faithful to His words!

WHEN YOU ARE TROUBLED

- Call upon me in the day of trouble; I will deliver you, and you will honor me. Psalm 50:15

- Do not be anxious about anything, but in everything, by prayer and petition, with thanksgiving, present your requests to God. And the peace of God, which transcends all understanding, will guard your hearts and your minds in Christ Jesus. Philippians 4:6-7

- Cast thy burden upon the Lord, and He shall sustain

thee: He shall never suffer the righteous to be moved. Psalms 55:22

- Come to me, all you who are weary and burdened, and I will give you rest. Matthew 11:28

- In this world, you will have trouble. But take heart! I have overcome the world! John 16:33

- I am with you and will watch over you wherever you go, and I will bring you back to this land. I will not leave you until I have done what I have promised. Genesis 28:15

- Some trust in chariots and some in horses, but we trust in the name of the Lord our God. Psalm 20:7

- I am the Lord, your God, who takes hold of your right hand and says to you, Do not fear; I will help you. Isaiah 41:13

- Trust in the Lord with all your heart and lean not on your own understanding; in all your ways acknowledge him, and he will make your paths straight. Proverbs 3:5-6

- He tends his flock like a shepherd: He gathers the lambs in his arms and carries them close to his heart; he gently leads those that have young. Isaiah 40:11

- Praise be to the Lord, to God our Savior, who daily bears our burdens. Psalm 68:19

- And we know that God causes all things to work together for good...He who did not spare His own Son, but delivered Him up for us all, how will He not also with Him freely give us all things. Romans 8:28,32

- He will not allow your foot to be moved; He who keeps you will not slumber. Psalms 121:3

- The Lord is nigh unto all them that call upon Him, to all that call upon Him in truth. Psalms 145:18

- Therefore, I tell you, do not be anxious about your life, what you shall eat or what you shall drink, nor about your body, what you shall put on. Is not life more than food, and the body more than clothing? Look at the birds of the air: they neither sow nor reap nor gather into barns, and yet your heavenly Father feeds them. Are you not of more value than they? And which of you by being anxious can add one cubit to his span of life? Matthew 6:25-27

WHEN YOU NEED PROSPERITY

- I will send down showers in season; there will be showers of blessing. Ezekiel 34:26

- He who did not spare his own Son, but gave him up for us all-how will he not also, along with him, graciously give us all things? Romans 8:32

- He satisfies the thirsty and fills the hungry with good things. Psalm 107:9

- Tell the righteous it will be well with them, for they will enjoy the fruit of their deeds. Isaiah 3:10

- God is able to make all grace abound to you, so that

in all things at all times, having all you need, you will abound in every good work. (2 Corinthians 9:8)

- The Lord will guide you always; he will satisfy your needs in a sun-scorched land and will strengthen your frame. Isaiah 58:11

- The Lord is my shepherd, I shall lack nothing. Psalm 23:1

- Remember the Lord your God, for it is he who gives you the ability to produce wealth. Deuteronomy 8:18

- God will meet all your needs. Philippians 4:19

WHEN YOU NEED COMFORT

- The Lord Almighty is with us; the God of Jacob is our fortress. Psalm 46:7

- From everlasting to everlasting the Lord's love is with those who fear him. Psalm 103:17

- Neither death nor life, neither angels nor demons, neither the present nor the future, nor any powers, neither height nor depth, nor anything else in all creation, will be able to separate us from the love of God that is in Christ Jesus our Lord. Romans 8:38-39

- Be strong and courageous. Do not be afraid or terrified because of them, for the Lord your God goes with you; he will never leave you nor forsake you. Deuteronomy 31:6

- Though my father and mother forsake me, the Lord will receive me. Psalm 27:10

- Surely I will be with you always, to the very end of the age. Matthew 28:20

WHEN YOU ARE FEELING CONFUSED

- Whoever follows me will never walk in darkness, but will have the light of life. John 8:12

- If any of you lacks wisdom, he should ask God, who gives generously to all without finding fault, and it will be given to him. James 1:5

- I will counsel you and watch over you. Psalm 32:8

- The Holy Spirit will teach you at that time what you should say. Luke 12:12

- The entrance of your words gives light; it gives understanding to the simple. Psalm 119:130

- Open my eyes that I may see wonderful things in your law. Psalm 119:18

WHEN YOU FEEL ILL

- I will heal my people and will let them enjoy abundant peace and security. Jeremiah 33:6

- Is any one of you sick? he should call the elders of the church to pray over him and anoint him with oil in the name of the Lord. And the prayer offered in faith will make the sick person well; the Lord will raise him up. James 5:14-15

- Heal me, O Lord, and I will be healed; save me and I will be saved, for you are the one I praise. Jeremiah 17:14

- Worship the Lord your God, and his blessing will be on your food and water. I will take away sickness from among you, and none will miscarry or be barren in your land. I will give you a full life span. Exodus 23:25-26

- I have seen his ways, but I will heal him; I will guide him and restore comfort to him. Isaiah 57:18

PROMISES OF LONG LIFE

- Ye shall walk in all the ways which the Lord your God hath commanded you, that ye may live, and that it may be well with you, and that ye may prolong your days in the land which ye shall possess. Deuteronomy 5:33

- That thou mightest fear the Lord thy God, to keep all his statutes, and his commandments, which I command thee; thou, and thy son, and thy son's son, all the days of thy life, and that thy days may be prolonged. Deuteronomy 6:2

- Thou shalt come to thy grave in a full age like as a shock of corn cometh in his season. Job 5:26

- What man is he that desireth life, and loveth many

days, that he may see good? Keep thy tongue from evil, and thy lips from speaking guile. Depart from evil, and do good; seek peace, and pursue it. Psalm 34:12, 14

- With long life will I satisfy him, and show him my salvation. Psalm 91:16

- Length of days, and long life, and peace, shall they add to thee. Length of days is in her [Wisdom's] right hand. Proverbs 3:2, 16

- By me thy days shall be multiplied, and the years of thy life shall be increased. Proverbs 9:11

- The fear of the Lord prolongeth days. Proverbs 10:27

PROMISES OF PEACE

- And I will give peace in the land, and ye shall lie down, and none shall make you afraid; and I will rid evil beasts out of the land, neither shall the sword go through your land. Leviticus 26:6.

- The Lord will give strength unto his people; the Lord will bless his people with peace. Psalm 29:11.

- Great peace have they which love thy law, and nothing shall offend them. Psalm 119:165.

- My people shall dwell in a peaceable habitation, and in sure dwellings, and in quiet resting-places. Isaiah 32:18

PROMISES OF FRUIT OF THE WOMB

- He will love thee, and bless thee, and multiply thee; he will also bless the fruit of thy womb. Deuteronomy 7:13.

- And the Lord thy God will make thee plenteous in the fruit of thy body. Deuteronomy 30:9.

- Thou shalt know also that thy seed shall be great, and thine offspring as the grass of the earth. Job 5:25.

- Lo, children are a heritage of the Lord; and the fruit of the womb is his reward. As arrows are in the hand of a mighty man, so are children of the youth. Happy is the man that hath his quiver full of them: they shall not be ashamed, but they shall speak with the enemies in the gate. Psalm 127:3-5.

- The Lord shall increase you more and more, you and your children. Psalm 115:14.

ABOUT YEMI OYINKANSOLA

Yemi Oyinkansola, a professional banker, called into full-time ministry, is a teacher and an encourager, with deep spiritual insight. He is a worshipper and prayer warrior who believes that all things are possible through God when one engages in intensive worship and fervent prayer through faith.

For his service and commitment to the East Bay community of California in 2017. He also received the Prestigious Special U.S Congressional Recognition Award by the Honorable Barbara Lee of 13th Congressional District of California.

Pastor Oyinkansola is the senior pastor of Jesus House Antioch, a branch of The Redeemed Christian Church of God in California, USA, where he resides with his beautiful wife, Comfort, and two lovely children, Melody and Toluwani.

Covenant Keeper, Not a Covenant Breaker

Yemi Oyinkansola

Covenant Keeper, Not a Covenant Breaker

www.ingramcontent.com/pod-product-compliance
Lightning Source LLC
LaVergne TN
LVHW051847080426
835512LV00018B/3124